D1470575

TEXAS WOMAN'S UNIVERSITY LIBRARY

The Art of Central Asia

Khiva, Tash-hauli Palace

Miloš Hrbas — Edgar Knobloch

The Art of Central Asia

Paul Hamlyn • London

Graphic design by Miloš Hrbas
Translated by Roberta Finlayson-Samsour
Designed and produced by Artia for
Paul Hamlyn Ltd
Westbook House · Fulham Broadway · London
© 1965 by Artia
Printed in Czechoslovakia

That part of Central Asia which is roughly bounded by the rivers Syr-Darya and Amu-Darya, the Aral Sea and the Tien-shan Mountains, has never been a coherent cultural region. This was due, on the one hand, to the character of the region — scattered oases, separated from one another by steppes and desert, developing more or less independently — and, on the other, to the fact that this relatively sparsely populated region was wedged throughout its history between three well-defined cultural entities — Persia, India and China, whose influences continually crossed and mingled.

The agriculture has always depended on artificial irrigation, the rivers providing a permanent water supply, fed from the glaciers of Tien-shan, the Pamirs and the Hindu Kush. The prosperity of the oases and their political and cultural importance depended to a large degree on passing trade — the flood of merchandise which from time immemorial had flowed through from the Ganges and the Indus to the Volga, and from China to Persia and on to the Mediterranean and Black Sea ports.

This trade fluctuated considerably, often for remote reasons, and the effects of these fluctuations were inevitably reflected in the life of Central Asia.

Fertile oases and the relative prosperity of a settled community of farmers and artisans often attracted raids by nomadic tribes from the steppes. Wave after wave of them emerged from the plains of Southern Siberia, from Mongolia and elsewhere, murdering the inhabitants, destroying their irrigation systems, so that the caravans were obliged to change their routes. So from earliest times, the cultural development of the region was linked with two opposing forces — the mature, organized and civilized states on the one hand, and the primitive, barbarian peoples on the other. These two conflicting streams are clearly expressed in the art of the region; sometimes they intermingle in a remarkable way, the influence of the civilized countries predominating in the towns, whereas in the country the traditions of the steppes persisted.

We are thus dealing with a territory whose inhabitants live the inward-looking life of a remote community linked with other settlements of the same kind by the fragile threads of the caravan routes. Handicrafts, except for pottery, brick-making and weaving, depended on the import of raw materials. The soil of the oasis was *loess*, a deposit of fine wind-transported dust, porous and very fertile under irrigation. Mining took place only in mountainous areas. The only building material was clay — wood was scarce and stone almost non-existent. Consequently the buildings were not particularly durable, sun-baked brick being less resistant to weathering, fire, or earthquake than stone, nor did the *loess* provide a substantial foundation. In certain places, such as low-lying Khwarazm, there was the additional menace of a high water level. Wind, sand and salt hastened the deterioration of the fabric. On the other hand, the dry air, the porous soil and sand have preserved many buried remains intact which still await investigation. The settlements are not only remote but numerous too, and in most cases only exploratory surveys have been carried out. Detailed work has been done by Professor Masson in Nessa (Parthia), by Professor Shishkin in Afrasiyab (ancient Samarkand) and by Professor Tolstov on the site of the palace-fortress Toprak-Kala (ancient Khwarazm). Our knowledge of Soviet Central Asia's past is therefore fragmentary and often dependent on outside sources.

In ancient times a large part of Central Asia was divided into the three outer satrapies of the Achaemenian empire of Persia: *Bactria* on the middle Amu, *Sogdiana* (Soghd) on the Zarafshan, and *Chorasmia* (Khwarazm) on the lower Amu near the Aral Sea. The remaining territory was inhabited by nomadic Scythian tribes, of whom the Masagetae, holding a large area east of the Aral Sea, were the most powerful. Cyrus sent a military expedition there and established the Sixteenth (Khwarazm) Satrapy. The first substantial clashes in the area were therefore between Persians and Scythian Masagetae. Then in the 4th century B.C., the expedition of Alexander of Macedonia, retreating through Bactria and Soghd to the banks of the Syr-Darya (or Jaxartes) river, introduced Hellenistic influences.

The Masagetian art of this time displays the characteristics of the well-known zoomorphic style of the Scythian *tumuli* in the region reaching from the Altai range to the southern Ukraine. Diez, in his *Iranische Kunst*, dates the rise of this style to ancient Soghd. Achaemenian Persia brought new elements stemming from the Near East, especially Assyria. The ornament of the period had a varied series of motifs, of which some, for instance the lotus leaf, are common to the whole ancient Orient, others such as rosettes and acanthus leaves indicate a western provenance, whereas a number, such as the palmette, can be regarded as indigenous. Some scholars, Rempel for example, (see Bibliography, page 27), see in the scroll and spiral a direct connexion with ram's horns, elements which reflect the nomadic, pastoral life of the steppes.

1. Soghd statuette, Samarkand; height 5 cm. Early 1st century. Tashkent Museum

Greek influence is obvious in the fantastic animals and mythological figures, winged lions, centaurs, medusas. Zoroastrianism has left clear traces in the repeated motif of the sun and in figurines of Ardvisura Anahit, the goddess of the waters, which were broken at an annual festival as symbolic sacrifices to the gods of fertility (plates 12-13).

The Greeks held sway in Bactria for over one and a half centuries. The Hellenistic states, Bactria and Seleucid Persia fought for many years against the kingdom of Parthia, along the south-east shore of the Caspian Sea. In this struggle, the Parthians had as their allies the Masagetian tribes between the Syr-Darya and the Aral Sea. The Greeks, too, sought support among nomadic tribes and enlisted the Huns, of Eastern Turkestan. In Eastern (Chinese) Turkestan, Turkish and Indo-European tribes lived side by side (the latter including the Iranian Saks and Soghds, and the Tokhars, whose language belongs to the western Indo-European group). Under pressure from the Huns, other tribes were displaced. The Saks, pushed on by the Tokhars, penetrated into Bactria and overthrew Greek rule. They ultimately settled in what is now South Afghanistan (Sistan). The main trade route from China to the west — the Silk Route — had at that time two branches: a northern route which led from Turfan in Eastern Turkestan to Ferghana and on to Samarkand, where it again divided, one road leading to the south and south-east over the Afghan passes into the Indus basin, the other continuing in a west to south-west direction into Persia, Iraq and the Caucasus. The southern branch of the main route skirted the southern part of the Takla Makan Desert, by way of Khotan and Yarkand, over the Pamir passes into Kabul and Herat, with a branch route in Khotan crossing the Karakoram Mountains into Kashmir and India. Both routes, however, had a number of alternatives, the choice of which was determined by climate, local politics, the safety and state of the roads, and by the level of water in the wells. It is interesting that all the incursions made by the raiders from the steppes followed fairly closely the direction of these caravan routes.

After the overthrow of Greek Bactria, the territory was settled by Tokhars (Tokharistan). At about the beginning of our era there arose in the oases on the Zarafshan a new centre of political power — the kingdom of Kushan. The rulers of Kushan extended their territories southwards. In the course of the 1st century A.D., they pushed their frontiers as far as the Indus and even farther, to Benares. And though the Kushanites made considerable territorial gains to the north-west, notably with the annexation of Khwarazm, the centre of gravity of their empire was shifted closer to the Indus and its capital became Purushapuram (now Peshawar). At the turn of the 1st and 2nd centuries, under King Kanishka, the Kushan state reached the height of its power, and stood on an equal footing with the greatest empires of the contemporary world — China, Parthia and Rome.

Indian traditions acquired increasing importance in the Kushan

Empire: Buddhism became the state religion, spreading along the silk routes into Eastern Turkestan and China. Kushan ('Gandhara') art, combining Indian and Hellenistic elements, penetrated with Buddhism into Central Asia and, until the arrival of Islam, was one of the most significant ingredients of the art of the region. Compared with this, the Chinese penetration to the Aral Sea, in the course of Kanishka's wars for domination of Eastern Turkestan, was of short duration and left few traces.

The Kushan Empire had declined by the middle of the third century, and there grew up on the ruins of Parthia a new Persia under the Sassanian dynasty. During these changes of fortune the territory of Khwarazm acquired independence, its chief centre at the turn of the third and fourth centuries being most probably the city and fortress on the right bank of the Lower Amu, today buried beneath the sands of the Kizyl Kum Desert and known to us as Toprak-Kala.

II. Soghd statuette, Varakhsha; height 6 cm. 5th century. Tashkent Museum

Khwarazm was, like the rest of the region, a country with a mature urban civilization. Tolstov's excavations of Toprak-Kala, carried out in 1947-50, revealed a surprisingly highly developed ancient civilization, of which nothing had been known until then. The city, occupying an area of 500 × 300 metres, was surrounded by earth ramparts, with watch-towers built of large rectangular bricks. In one corner stood the great royal palace, with three towers, beside it a temple (probably dedicated to the Holy Fire) and a large market place. The inhabitants dwelt in 10-12 large house blocks of 100-200 rooms, divided by lanes and disposed along the axis of the main street. Tolstov concentrated his digging on the royal palace, where he found fragments of highly characteristic frescoes and sculpture, books written on wood and on leather, glazed pottery, coins and arms. Tolstov's findings at Toprak-Kala all date from the 3rd to the 5th centuries, the palace itself being presumably destroyed at the end of the 3rd century (plates 17-21).

The archaeological evidence from Toprak-Kala and other Khwarazm towns points to a knowledge of metal-work, and to specialized handicrafts of high quality. The dense population provided sufficient labour for the installation and maintenance of irrigation systems, a requisite of prosperous agriculture. In the towns the people kept to their own specialized skills, and trade in a variety of commodities flourished.

Trade routes were predominately overland. Trade by sea existed (see *The Travels of the Chinese Pilgrim Fa Sien*, written in the 5th century), but it seems to have been limited and risky. Active communications must have existed between the harbours of India, Indonesia and China and, perhaps to a lesser degree, along the coast of the Persian Gulf, South Arabia and East Africa. The Chinese, Javanese and Singhalese vessels were quite large. A Han dynasty source refers to ships with several masts and as many as five decks (quinqueremes).

At the beginning of the 5th century tribes from outlying regions began to exert pressure on Central Asia. White Huns (Ephthalites), emerged

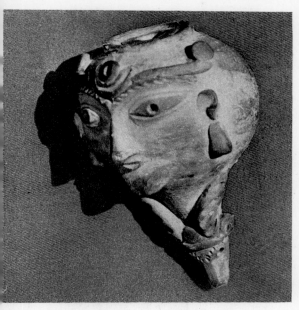

III. Ephthalite sculpture, Varakhsha; height 10 cm. 6th century. Samarkand Museum

from the marshy flats between the Aral Sea and the Syr-Darya, and easily overcame the small Soghd principalities. They then came into conflict with the Sassanian Persians who had penetrated Central Asia from the south-west. Persia defended herself in a long and costly campaign. The Ephthalites penetrated deep into India, occupied Eastern Turkestan, largely restoring the original Kushan empire. Their dominion did not last long, but made a deep split in the cultural life of the country. In the Ephthalite, and similarly in the succeeding Turkish period, Soghd art comes very close to South Siberia and the Altai. The influence of the steppe peoples permeated the former cultural tradition, replacing certain elements, and giving new life to others. The classical architectural features (capitals, friezes) disappear and the refined and carefully wrought sculptures are replaced by coarse representations in archaic style. On coins, realistic portraits give way to the primitively incised features of barbarian chieftains (Rempel). On the other hand, numerous craftsmen arrived from Tokharistan and Iran, seeking asylum from religious persecution (Manichaeans, Nestorians) and they brought techniques and decorative elements from their own countries. Under the Ephthalites, the Soghds settled along the trade routes in distant Eastern Turkestan, spreading their Central Asian culture.

Ancient towns of the Toprak-Kala type slowly fell into decay after the breaking up of the Kushan kingdom. The aristocracy fortified their country residences, which then became the centres of commercial and artistic life. The most notable finds from the Ephthalite and Turkish periods are from the strongholds of Varakhsha, not far from Bukhara. In the sixth decade of the 6th century the Ephthalites were overcome by the western Turks, whose original settlements were in the steppes of South Siberia. The destruction of Ephthalite power prompted a Chinese invasion from the east, and eventually the Turkish hordes were defeated by Chinese forces. For a short time, Central Asia became part of the Chinese empire.

Central Asia presented at this time a rich variety of creeds. The original ancient religion of Zarathustra still survived and, from the time of the Kushans, Buddhism was also strongly represented. The hostile attitude of the Ephthalites to the latter religion undermined its position both in Central Asia and in India. From the 6th century Buddhism was thus in decline, its place being taken by the teachings of the Persian philosopher and reformer, Manes (Manichaeism). Nomadic tribes introduced the animistic conceptions of tribal shamanism, and Christianity made its contribution, for Nestorian faith was even preached in Eastern Turkestan. In the second half of the 7th century, however, a new conquest wiped out almost immediately every opposing faith, substituting for them a new, militant religion, closely bound up with temporal power. The Arabs overthrew the Persian Sassanian empire, occupied Khorasan and penetrated as far as the Syr-Darya and Ferghana. Islam became the state religion and the sole source of artistic inspiration, a function it fulfilled for a full twelve centuries. Khwarazm suffered particularly. This country, whose prosperity had been declining since the incursions of the Ephthalites, lost at one blow all its trade links, for the Arabs naturally reorientated all trade towards the centre of their empire, that is, to Iraq and the Persian Gulf. The havoc of war was also considerable, one of the consequences being a drastic reduction of the irrigation network. The urban culture of Khwarazm had practically ceased to exist by the 8th and 9th centuries, its place being taken by a system of scattered strongholds and open villages. However, the caliphs did not govern directly in Central Asia. As at the time of the Persian empire, this territory retained some independence, the chiefs being administratively subordinate to the caliph's governor in Merv. Gradually, as the power of the Baghdad caliphs decreased, the ties between the territorial chiefs and the empire slackened and their independence grew. By the end of the 9th and the beginning of the 10th century, several of them had thrown off all allegiance to Baghdad.

One of the outstanding political entities on the eastern border of the Arab empire was the state of the Samanids, with its centre in Bukhara, which in the first half of the 10th century occupied the greater part of Central Asia. In Khwarazm two petty states arose, the westerly one (with its main power centre in Urganch-Gurganj) engaging in brisk trade with the Khazar empire, in the South Ukraine.

Along the northern borders of these states stretched the territories of the semi-nomadic Turkic Oghuz. At this time Kiev Russia extended from the west to the Volga. In its struggle with the Khazars, the Oghuz became allies of the Russians, whereas Khwarazm was on the side of the Khazars. This was the first direct contact between Central Asia and Europe. The political influence of Islam was so strong in the still pagan Russian empire that Prince Vladimir for a time hesitated between Christianity or Islam, that is, between Byzantium and Baghdad.

Turkish tribes were a constant threat to the south, in the region of the

IV—V. Laboratory glass ware, 10th century. Tashkent Museum

14

great river basins. At the end of the 10th century the Samanid empire collapsed under the pressure of the Turkish dynasty of the Kara-khanids, whose nucleus of power was Uzkend on the Kara-Darya now in the Kirghiz S. S. R.). The rule of the Kara-khanids was soon brought to an end by incursions of southern Turks, under the sultans of Ghazni (now in Eastern Afghanistan). The Seljuks, however, at the turn of the millennium, suppressed the Ghaznevid empire, conquered Iran and, finally, brought Baghdad under their domination. The Abbasid caliphs became mere puppets in the hands of their Seljuk overlords.

Islam brought fundamental changes to the art of Central Asia. The new faith brought with it a definite philosophy, rejected and denied the validity of all previous native religions and set up in their place a new, rigid and exclusive code, expressed in art by a complete and comprehensive set of forms.

The clash between the highly civilized peoples and the more primitive tribes from the steppes, however, also left its mark on Islamic art. Islam first established itself in the urban centres, while in the country the older customs and traditions prevailed. Geometric and floral motifs, typical of Islamic ornament, are still rare outside the towns; on the other hand, Zoroastrian and Manichaean motifs and representational elements (the sun, moon, and stars, sacred trees, animal symbols, etc.) still persist and form a link between the old Soghd art and the art of Islam. The feudal towns which had sprung up since the 9th century at the cross-roads of the caravan routes and in other profitable places, initiated a new style of art, particularly in architecture and ornament.

The mediaeval town of Central Asia was traditionally composed of three parts: the centre was usually the fortified palace (*ark*, *kala*) surrounded by ramparts, usually of clay, occasionally of brick. In some places such as Khiva, the ring of fortifications enclosed the whole inner part of the town. The fortress formed the core round which the town (*medina*, *shahristan*) grew up. In some cases this was from the outset on a regular ground plan — with streets radiating from the centre or on a rectangular plan — and surrounded by a second zone of defences. Beyond the ramparts were the suburbs, gardens, etc. The town's water-supply came from irrigation channels (*aryks*) carrying water from the river or from reservoirs (*hauz*). Various parts of the town were given over to particular trades, where commodities were both manufactured and sold; the streets were shaded by reed mats or with canvas awnings. Where the shopping streets crossed, they were roofed with brick cupolas, in some places preserved to this day.

No buildings remain from the first centuries of the Islamic era. All that remains of the period between the 10th and the 14th centuries are four types of sacred edifice (mosques, minarets, mausolea and madrasas), but no secular buildings.

The main elements of each building (minarets excepted) were the cupola and the *ivan*. The brick cupola was the natural form of roofing in

VI. Dish, imitation porcelain; diameter 30 cm. 15th century. Samarkand Museum

a country with a chronic lack of timber. The interiors were therefore of limited size. In an attempt to enlarge the interior, the cupola was raised on a drum. The most notable building of this kind is the mausoleum of Timur Beg (Tamerlane), at Gur-Emir in Samarkand (plates 79-80). The *ivan* is the open-vaulted hall, or the niche of the portico, variously articulated and richly decorated. In the monuments of Timur the Lame, as Tamerlane is also called, the *ivans* acquired immense dimensions as in the Bibi-khanum Mosque. The entrance gateway is 19.30 metres high, the main building 17 metres, (see fig. IX and plate 81). Aq-saray, in Shahrisabz is 22. 2 metres high (see plate 88). The Throne Rooms of the Khivan Khans (the Tash-hauli Palace, plates 122 and 123) are basically *ivans*, in which the vault was replaced by a slight timber framing filled in with reed mats, supported on one or two wooden pillars. The private houses of Khiva still have *ivans* today (locally pronounced: *aivans*), supported on a single pillar. In winter quarters the *ivan* faces south, and, in summer quarters, an *ivan* of double the height, faces north, drawing the cool air inwards to the courtyard.

The old Arab mosques had rectangular courtyards, surrounded by walls and a colonnade. In the course of time and with changing climatic conditions the rows of columns were transformed into covered arcades to give shade within the courtyard, and above the niche *(mihrab)* a domed structure was raised. Still later the mosque came to be an enclosed building, with a dome and a massive portal extending to the whole breadth of the façade. The courtyard with a number of parallel arcades is still preserved in the groundplan of the Bukhara mosque, known as the Masjid-i-Kalan, dating from the 12th century, the main domed structure of which was restored in the 15th and 16th centuries. Similarly, the Bibi-khanum Mosque in Samarkand (1399-1404) is reminiscent, with its arcades and courtyard, of the original mosque with columns.

In Central Asia, the minaret *(manara)* is usually circular and tapering (Turan type), unlike its Arab counterpart. The finest and best preserved examples are from pre-Mongolian times, in the city of Bukhara (plates 51-53) and in Vabkent near Bukhara (fig. VII).

The madrasa, or theological college, consisted usually of an inner courtyard surrounded by one-storey buildings, in which were situated a mosque, lecture-rooms, and the living quarters of the pupils and teachers. In the middle of each wall there was usually a decorated doorway. The walls looking onto the street were blind, later being decorated with niches (plates 92, 107).

The mausoleum *(mazar — a grave)* is a domed structure raised over the grave of a distinguished person. The oldest preserved mausoleums of the Samanid Ismail, in Bukhara (beginning of the 10th century, plate 41), and of the Seljuk sultan Sanjar, in Merv (12th century), are still simple cube-shaped structures, with no portico. The Ismail mauso-

VII. Minaret in Vabkent near Bukhara, 1196-8

VIII. Dish, glazed pottery; diameter 25 cm. 2nd half of the 14th century. Samarkand Museum

X. Samarkand, Bibi-khanum Mosque, south-west
iew of main building

leum is relatively small (outer edge 9.30 metres, inner edge 7.20 metres, height 9 metres). The brick cupola is raised over eight arches, four of which span the inner walls, four intersecting them at the corners. The Kara-khanid mausolea in Uzkend, however, already represent a new type of structure, with an imposing portico. The central building dating from the 11th century, is now in ruins. Discernible on the remains of the façade is a somewhat primitive terracotta ornament and, inside, a band of remarkably fine carved plaques, with what are clearly pre-Islamic motifs. Of the cupola only the corner vault remains (plates 43 and 44). Both the north and south of the Uzkend mausolea had a portico, richly decorated in carved terracotta with bands of ornament. The elaborate articulation of the entrance arch or *ivan* and the ornamentation, served as a pattern for future masterpieces in Timur's Shah-i-Zinda (plates 45-50). The ornament of early Islam was influenced, on the one hand, by religious prescriptions and, on the other, by the standards of building technique. Alabaster carving, which had formerly decorated the sun-baked walls of buildings, no longer served the same purpose now that prefabricated bricks became the main building material. The wall decoration was based on geometric shapes of the bricks themselves, the dimensions of the brick forming the basic unit. Arabesques (*girikh*) of intertwining figures, constructed on grids with the help of ruler and compasses appear in plates 46, 47, 54. The basic figure is a square inscribed within a circle. From this figure octagons, hexagons, six or eight-rayed stars and any other figures with straight lines can be constructed. These units can then be extended to cover the whole surface of a wall in many combinations. There are also the more complicated radial grids on a squared foundation, and triangular grids, or grids for the curving surfaces of cupolas and vaults.

The development of geometric ornament and, indeed, of the whole art of architecture from the 9th-12th centuries, is bound up with the advance of Arabic mathematics (al-Khwarizmi, al-Farabi and others). Another independent type of ornament is the free-drawn repeat ornament with plant motifs. This derives from observation of nature, in the same way as the geometrical ornament derived from an exact calculation of the space and construction of the motif.

The old motifs of acanthus leaves, rosettes, palmettes, spirals, etc. were given new expression. They were stylized and symmetrically arranged within a prescribed area. This *islimi* ornament based on a pattern of stems, spirals and scrolls, with leaves and flowers flatly rendered, usually supplements the geometrical ornament on smaller surfaces (backgrounds, arch surfaces, etc.).

Special figures derive from applying geometric principles to simple curving elements. These fall into three groups, *madokhils*, where the surface is covered with figures of a single type; medallions, used to punctuate the main geometrical surfaces (areas covered with designs without repeats), and various kinds of border.

. Dish, imitation porcelain; diameter 30 cm.
5th century. Samarkand Museum

17

Frequently Islamic ornament is combined with calligraphic script. The oldest *ductus* of Arabic writing, the *kufic*, with its stiff, angular forms, was well suited to contrast with geometrical ornament. The combination of vegetal motifs with *kufic*, gave rise to what is known as 'foliated *kufic*'. A desire to enrich the decoration even further produced plaited and interlaced *kufic* (plates 47, 48). In the 11th and 12th centuries the *kufic* script was superseded by the more decorative *naskhi* (plate 49), from which evolved the highly cursive *thulth* (plate 59). *Kufic* was still used for inscriptions on large surfaces, where it was possible to compose them directly from whole bricks or glazed tiles (plate 77), *naskhi* and *thulth* being limited to inscriptions of smaller dimensions, on the arches of doorways and so on.

Ornament is everywhere in Islamic art, in ceramics and textiles, in metal and wood-work, but most of all in architecture. The fact that religion prohibited representational painting and sculpture, explains the use of ornament as the only form of artistic expression apart from architecture. The techniques for decorating buildings varied: the simplest was the previously mentioned arrangement of bricks in such a way as to form regular figures (the Ismail Mausoleum in Bukhara, plate 42, and the Kalan Minaret in Vabkent near Bukhara). At the beginning of the 12th century the use of ceramic tiles as a wall-covering was introduced, the tiles being glazed pale blue and red, as, for example, on the Kalan Minaret. This technique did not reach its height until the end of the 14th century. Another method was to draw patterns in soft mud, which was then baked — incised terracotta — as at the Uzkend Mausoleum (plates 46-50), and the Magoki Attari Mosque in Bukhara (plate 54). Inside, the walls were covered with incised alabaster, a practice surviving from earlier times. Incised, unglazed terracotta was widely used during the second half of the 12th and the beginning of the 13th century. Khwarazm, again united at the end of the 10th century, became an important centre of Islamic science and scholarship, just as Spanish Córdova did, a century later, at the opposite end of the Islamic empire. Khwarazmshah Abu-l'Abbas al-Mamun actually founded at his court in Gurganj an academy, whose distinguished members included, among others, al-Biruni and Ibn Sina (Avicenna). Arabic science also made possible a rapid development of trade. Advances in shipbuilding and especially in navigation resulted in a large part of international trade being transferred, from the beginning of the 8th century, to sea routes. The Indian Ocean became 'the Arabian Sea' and Arab merchants and sailors made regular voyages to East India, Indonesia and China, as well as along the East African coast, as far as Sofala in Mozambique. This change of trade routes, combined with the confused political situation, was the cause of the decay of the Central Asian cities in the 11th and 12th centuries.

Not until the second half of the 12th century, with the further decline of the power of the caliphs, did Central Asia experience a short period of consolidation under the rule of the Seljuk sultans resident in Khwarazm. Owing to the growth of trade with Russia, the Khwarazm state enjoyed temporary prosperity at the end of the 12th and beginning of the 13th century. At this time the Khwarazmshahs brought under their dominion the remains of the empire of the Kara-khanids and governed the whole territory between the Amu and the Syr-Darya (Arabic Mawara'n-Nahr).

Besides Gurganj, which now became a real metropolis, a number of other towns grew up and flourished; the area under irrigation was again extended and the population increased rapidly. A feudal system prevailed at this period. At the head of the hierarchy were the Turkish conquerors, and there was a deep rift between the Turks and the native inhabitants, causing a lack of stability, so that when the Khwarazm empire was seriously put to the test, it fell easily.

The incursion of Jenghiz-Khan's Mongols in 1220 spelt not only the end of the political existence of Khwarazm, but the complete disruption of Central Asian economy and cultural life. Whole regions were depopulated, cities burnt down, dams and irrigation channels destroyed. Only very few architectural monuments survived. Worse still, as a result of the Mongolian invasion, the direction of the great trade routes was changed and a considerable number of once rich and flourishing oases were never thereafter resettled.

Just as the Ephthalites and Turks had in earlier times brought to an end the ancient Khwarazm civilization, now the Mongols, thanks to their mobility, organization and military tactics, systematically destroyed medieval Khwarazm. Then, a strong and united Persia had opposed the Ephthalites and halted further aggression, but now the Mongols met with little resistance from the weak and disintegrating state of the Abbasid caliphs. In 1258 a second wave of Mongol raiders destroyed Baghdad, and the whole great civilization of the Islamic Orient lay in ruins.

Overland trade was disrupted until the Mongols consolidated their dominions by turning them into more closely-knit states. The rise of the Golden Horde on the Volga, of the Chaghatay *ulus* in Central Asia, the empire of the Il-Khans in Persia and of Kublai-Khan in North China, created a demand for a revival of at least the principal trade routes, the restoration of the most important cities and the resettlement of oases. Until the Mongol invasion, Persia had always been the strongest influence on Central Asian countries. With the coming of the Mongols, these connexions were broken off and Iranian influence weakened in favour of the Turko-Mongolian power.

Timur's empire — the first large state to have its gravitational centre in Central Asia — was a direct result of the new political situation. In the second half of the 14th century Timur raised, on the ruins of the Chaghatay *ulus*, an empire which, as the result of thirty years of expansion, reached from India to the Caucasus and from the Persian Gulf to the Volga. Its capital was Samarkand, which Timur developed with care. Wide and active trade communications and stable living conditions brought prosperity to Samarkand, and with material prosperity, art and architecture flourished, too. Timur forcibly gathered together the best artists and craftsmen from his conquered territories, to embellish his cities. At the turn of the 14th and 15th centuries there was, as a result, a renaissance of Islamic art in Central Asia. After a long period of decay, high standards returned. On Arab-Persian foundations, works of art arose in which Turkish influence was important, and in which occasional Chinese, Indian, and Mongol elements appear.

A rapid advance was made especially in pottery techniques; unglazed terracotta practically disappears in the second half of the 14th century and its place is taken by glazed pottery, with an increasingly wide colour range. The old use of lead glazes which oxidized quickly, from pre-Mongolian times was replaced by durable glazes stained with colouring oxides. Thus iron oxides gave yellow, red, brown, black and grey glazes, copper oxides green and blue, chromium oxide dark green, cobalt salts blue glazes, etc. Addition of tin changed a transparent glaze into an opaque one. Conversely, the addition of ash from certain plants added lustre and transparency. Each colour had its own optimal firing temperature. A mosaic design of single-coloured tiles had the advantage of being simple to produce, but the ornamental design was limited to geometrical patterns based on the shape of the tiles, as was the case with the earlier ornament using unglazed tiles. This difficulty was then overcome by the technique of 'inlaid mosaic' composed of variously coloured small units. Painted majolica plates gave much greater scope, as regards design, but the precise shade of colour was very difficult to achieve. Painting could be carried out either beneath or on top of a ready-glazed surface.

In Samarkand, where the influence of incised terracotta from pre-Mongolian times was strongest, glazed incised terracotta appeared for the first time on the mausoleum of Khoja Ahmad, in the Shah-i-Zinda complex, (listed as No. 14 in the catalogue of buildings in the Shah-i-Zinda complex, and dating from 1320-1360). Also on this mausoleum are the glazed panels, with imitation mosaic (the geometrical pattern is in fact incised), and stamped tiles (the pattern is in low relief). Gilding, imitating local brocade embroideries, was the basis of what is known as *kundal* drawing, first used, too, in the Shah-i-Zinda complex, in the interior of the Kasim Mausoleum (building No. 16), and later in the interiors of the Bibi-khanum Mosque and the Gur-Emir Mausoleum, in the form of gilded painting on wallpapers composed of several layers of tissue paper.

In the repertoire of ornamental motifs, *girikh* yields to vegetal designs; it would seem that geometrical inventiveness had been exhausted in the previous period. The field is dominated by the *islimi* style, on the one hand, and by *madokhil* figures and medallions with stylized plant motifs, on the other, preference being given now to mosaic work, now to painted majolica. Colour combinations are of great importance, calculated with the same precision as were the geometrical figures of the preceding age. The new decoration was made more difficult in that the colour combinations were dependent on the limited glazing techniques available. Thus majolica is usually predominantly blue, whereas mosaics show a preference for red and green (see Rempel).

Colour gradation is used to give depth: the dark background receding most, the lighter colours bringing out successively the more important parts of the design, with white reserved for inscriptions and contours. The strength of colours used was also governed by whether the subject was to appear on bright or shaded surfaces, that is on an outside south wall, or a shadowy niche.

The Shah-i-Zinda group in Samarkand (plates 56-75), is a complex of sixteen buildings clustered along a seventy-metre path, of which the grave of the Muslim saint Kasim, at the northern end, is the focal point. Kasim, according to one tradition, was a relation of Muhammad's who fell here in battle at the time of the Arab invasion. According to another version, he was a hermit who lived in a cave on the site of his grave, round which arose the group of Kara-khanid mausolea, the 'Old Shah-i-Zinda'. Of these buildings little remains. In the years 1334-5 a mausoleum was raised above Kasim's grave and round it buildings were successively erected, forming the present Shah-i-Zinda (The Living King). The bad state of preservation and the absence of informative inscriptions has lead to a divergence of views as to the date and chronology of these buildings. In the plan in fig. XI the buildings are numbered 1-16, beginning with the entrance portico (No. 1) and ending with Kasim's Mausoleum (No. 16). Building 14, the portal of Khoja Ahmad, is, after Kasim's tomb, the oldest and the only remaining building of the Old Shah-i-Zinda (first half of the 14th century). Mausoleum 15 is dated 1360. Under Timur (1375-1405) arose mausolea 4-7 (Central Group I), mausolea 9-11 (Central Group II) and in the northern, top group, beyond the central portico, buildings 12 and 13. Central Group II is extensively damaged. It would appear that only members of Timur's family, including women, were buried in the mausolea. Dating from the reign of Timur's grandson Ulugh-beg (1409-1449), are the main entrance portico and the southern group of mausolea (Nos. 2 and 3 of the complex), as well as building 8, an open octagon which probably served as a minaret.

The mausolea of the central and northern groups are all quite small, and were built on a rectangular ground plan, with brick cupolas sometimes raised on a drum, and magnificently articulated porticos. The *ivan* in most cases, is covered with cellar or stalactite vaulting, with a rich ceramic tiling. Neither of the mausolea of the bottom group have porticos with an *ivan*, but their domes are raised on high drums (plate 56), as in the Gur-Emir Mausoleum. In the 18th century another mosque (not numbered in the plan — plate 109) was built behind the main portico.

Of Timur's architectural achievements at least three are outstanding. First and foremost there is Timur's royal palace of Aq-saray, in Shahri-sabz, one-time Kesh, south of Samarkand. All that remains of this great monument, of which a detailed description has been preserved in the report of the Castilian envoy, Gonzáles de Clavijo, from the year 1404, is part of the entrance gate, with an immense *ivan*. The flanking towers were at least 40 metres high. It is, with the exception of the remains of the palace in Tirmidh, the first secular building in Central Asia of which some part has been preserved (plates 84, 88). The Bibi-khanum Mosque, now badly damaged, is one of the largest buildings of its kind. Its inner court is 90 × 60 metres, the entrance gateway 41 metres, and the main building is 14.5 metres long. The cupola on a high drum has been is demolished (fig. IX, plates 76, 77, 81, 82).

Timur's mausoleum, Gur-Emir, represents the culmination of his building activities. Raised upon an octagonal base is a high drum covered with a ribbed dome. At the four corners were minarets of which only the remains still stand. Beneath the honeycombed vaulting of the main hall stand the cenotaphs of Timur, Ulugh-beg, and two of Timur's sons. The actual graves are in an underground crypt. The predominant colours of the tiles lining it are blue and gold (plates 78-80).

These crowning examples of Islamic architecture are distinguished by the fact that they are a great deal larger than other buildings of the same type, without there being any change in the ground plan or any increase in the number of storeys. Nor are the bricks any larger, as large mosaic designs of glazed tiles covered the façades. Little remains of the building activities of Ulugh-beg save an imposing madrasa in the market at Samarkand (plates 83, 89, 90), now in a poor state of preservation, and a smaller madrasa at Bukhara (plate 52).

The fifteenth century brought important changes. After Timur's death in 1405, the Empire declined and Samarkand was reduced to the level of a provincial town. Culturally it still flourished under Timur's grandson, Ulugh-beg, a distinguished scholar and astronomer, who died in 1449. Towards the end of his reign Samarkand again became for a short time the chief city of what remained of Timur's empire, while radical changes were taking place in the country's trade.

At the beginning of the 14th century the ancient caravan links between China and Central Asia were renewed. Chinese maritime trade which, under the Mongol emperors, had faded into the background, now returned in the first half of the 15th century with renewed vigour. Chinese merchants had stations strung out along the whole coast of India, and made regular voyages as far as the Persian Gulf and the coast of East Africa. As a result of internal affairs in China, a decisive change took place in about 1450. All maritime trade was brought to a halt, the building of ships (some as large as 700 tons) was prohibited and

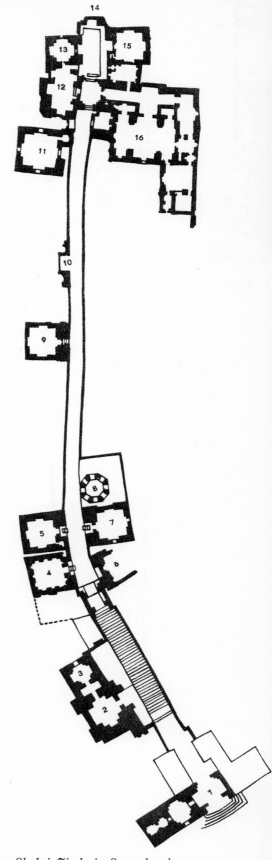

XI. Shah-i-Zinda in Samarkand

22

XII. Kokand, palace of Khudoyar-Khan, 1871, façade

maps were destroyed. China deliberately sealed herself off from the outside world. This naturally affected the caravan trade. In the second half of the 15th century the settlements along the trade routes lost their main source of prosperity. Trade across the Indian Ocean was soon taken over by Europeans — first the Portuguese and then the Dutch. Thus the whole orientation of the trade routes in this part of the world was changed and the Central Asian oases all at once found themselves on the periphery.

At the beginning of the 16th century there arose in Bukhara and in Khiva (on the territory of former Khwarazm) miniature states — khanates tributary to semi-nomadic Turks, joined in the 18th century by a third khanate, with its capital in Kokand, on the upper Syr-Darya. Their history presents a depressing picture of cultural backwardness, fanatical religious intolerance, internecine strife, xenophobia and complete isolation from external influences. When the Uzbeg khans of the Sheybanid dynasty conquered Herat in 1528, they brought with them to their capital city of Bukhara artists and craftsmen from Herat, and erected a number of outstanding buildings. From that time date the vaulted bazaars (plate 99), the attractive madrasa of Mir-i-Arab (plates 96-98, 102, 103) and, from somewhat later (the end of the 16th century), the large Kukeldash Madrasa, comprising 160 cells (plates 107, 108), and the Abdullah-Khan Mosque (plates 100, 101). At the same time the restoration was completed of the largest Central Asian mosque — the Masjid-i-Kalan. A marked decline can be observed in pottery techniques, and only two kinds maintained their standards: the panelling with mosaic work and the technique of glazed majolica. The colour range is often reduced to just two colours, a number of characteristic colours disappear altogether, and the remaining ones are muddy and dull. These shortcomings are due, above all, to a deterioration in the quality of the materials used for the glazes. The laws governing colour composition were ignored and the ornament shows a marked decline. The only innovations at this period are the Bukhara brick mosaics of the 16th century (bricks inlaid with alabaster), and the technique of colour alabaster. Here, two layers of alabaster were used, the design either being cut through a white surface to reveal the coloured ground, or incised into the white body and filled with coloured clay.

At the beginning of the 17th century the complex of the Registan in Samarkand was completed with two more notable buildings: the Shere-Dor Madrasa (plate 91) and the 'Golden' madrasa of Tilla Kari (plates 93-4), where the ceiling of the mosque used to be decorated in gold. This concludes the list of outstanding architectural monuments in Central Asia. All that was built in the 17-19th centuries was of secondary importance. Several examples of secular buildings, however, must be included; but the palaces of the Bukhara emirs (18th century — plates 104, 106) and of the Kokand khans (1871 — fig. XII, plate

110), both in their architecture and decoration, lag far behind the ruins of Timur's Aq-saray (White Palace) in Shahrisabz (Kesh).

Not until the end of the 18th century did the trade routes between Khiva and the Volga revive, when Russian capital was endeavouring to penetrate into the Central Asian markets. The consequence of this revival was a short, intensive period of artistic architectural activity in Khiva.

Within the precincts of the inner fortress (Ichan-Kala), and in the neighbourhood of the old palace (Kunya-Ark, 18th century), the imposing palace of Tash-hauli was erected in 1830-33, with three courtyards and six *ivans* of light construction, decorated with characteristic Khiva majolica in muted colours, mostly blues, and displaying a wide range of ornamental motifs. The majolica is of indifferent quality, the pattern lacks definition and there are inaccuracies in the drawing, but the architecture is distinguished by a purity and harmony of form.

The Khiva ornament, although a part of the Central European tradition, has an individual character which distinguishes it from other ornamental schemes. Only one group of the traditional *girikh* occurs here — star shaped figures inscribed within pentagons. By extending the straight lines of these forms, new patterns of *girikh* arise which are not to be found anywhere else. The plant or flower patterns at Khiva represent the crowning achievement of Central Asian ornament; even if it falls short of the Bukhara ornament from the point of view of technique, it surpasses it in the rich variety of its motifs. The Bukhara ornament evolves from architecture, and influences all forms of artistic expression. In Khiva, on the contrary, ornamentation is an imposed, separate feature, and the common motifs persist in the majolica and the carving, the textiles and the metal-work.

XIII. Khwarazm, folk ornament on wall of a hauli

XIV. Khwarazm, country house or hauli

XV. Samarkand carpet, 19th century. Samarkand Museum

An integral part of every *ivan* is the carved wooden pillar typical of Khwarazm architecture of early times. In 1835 a mausoleum was erected in Khiva to the local saint, Pahlavan Mahmud, of which the octagonal dome raised over a rectangular ground plan represents the third type of mausoleum, chronologically the latest and seen particularly in Iran (plates 119-120, 128-129). Somewhat later is the large madrasa of Muhammad Amin Khan; the minaret, Kalta Minar, of 1850, remained uncompleted, interesting features being the unusually large diameter and the predominance of green and yellow in the colour scheme (plates 127, 139). The Khoja Islam minaret, completed in 1908, is the last notable architectural achievement of the Islamic era in Central Asia (plates 137, 138). The almost perfectly preserved city fortifications in Khiva, with several gates, give an excellent idea of the military architecture of the time.

The country houses in Khwarazm, known as *hauli* (fig. XIV), form a particular type of domestic architecture. They were traditionally constructed as miniature strongholds for protection against robbers — reminiscent of the time when conditions were unsettled and the threat of raids frequent. The actual house, with its small courtyard and *ivan* (see above, p. 16), is surrounded by high earth ramparts with battlements and massive pilasters and, instead of the usual small postern, a strongly fortified gateway. The surrounding wall was often decorated with folk ornaments (fig. XIII), the motifs (circles, crosses, discs, palmettes and spirals) harking back to the prehistoric patterns of the nomads of the steppes. In nineteenth-century Khwarazm we see for the last time the traditional contrast between the nomad elements of the country (*hauli*), and the sophisticated art of monumental architecture and ornament (*girikh, islimi*) of the town.

AUTHOR'S NOTE

From early periods illustrating the development of art in pre-Islamic times, I have chosen only the most characteristic subjects. The same is true of the selected examples of local handicraft of later times. As regards architecture, some surviving buildings have been omitted, the Sanjar Mausoleum in Merv, for example. I hope, nevertheless, that this book can give the reader a general idea of the main architectural styles and ornament of Central Asia, and the influence which shaped their development.

I should also like to thank, first and foremost, the Czechoslovak Ministry of Schools and Culture and the State Commision for Cultural Relations attached to the Council of Ministers of the U.S.S.R. for enabling us to make the journey to Central Asia; the staff of the Museums of History and Art in Tashkent, the Regional Museums in Samarkand, Bukhara, Kokand and Khiva, who kindly placed their exhibits at our disposal; and to express our indebtedness to Professor Felix Tauer of the Philosophical Faculty of the Caroline University in Prague, Dr Věra Kubíčková-Stivínová of the Oriental Institute in Prague and Dr Jarmila Štěpková of the Náprstek Museum, Prague, for their assistance in selecting, classifying and identifying the material we brought back with us. A special acknowledgement, too, is due to Professor Felix Tauer for checking the data quoted in the text.

E. K.

BIBLIOGRAPHY

V. V. Barthold: *Turkestan v epokhu mongolskovo nashestviya*. Moscow, 1900

V. V. Barthold: *Turkestan down to the Mongol Invasion*. (Engl. trans.) London, 1928, 1958

K. Brockelmann: *Geschichte der islamischen Völker und Staaten*. Munich, 1939

E. Cohn-Wiener: *Turan*. Berlin, 1930

E. Diez: *Iranische Kunst*. Vienna, 1944

H. A. Giles (translator): *The Travels of Fa-Hsien, 399-414*. Cambridge, 1923

E. Kühnel: *Islamische Schriftkunst*. Berlin-Leipzig, 1942

V. Lesný: *Buddhismus*. Prague, 1948

S. N. Polupanov: *Arkhitekturnye pamyatniki Samarkanda* (Architectural Monuments of Samarkand), Moscow, 1948

L. I. Rempel: *Arkhitekturnyi ornament Uzbekistana* (The Architectural Ornament of Uzbekistan). Tashkent, 1961

A. Speltz: *Der Ornamentstil*. Leipzig, 1912

G. Le Strange: *The Lands of the Eastern Caliphate*. Cambridge, 1905

P. Sykes: *History of Afghanistan*. London, 1940

F. Tauer: *Dějiny a kultura islamu* (The History and Culture of Islam). Prague, 1940

S. P. Tolstov: *Po sledam drevniekhorezmskoi tsivilizatsii* (On the Track of the Ancient Civilization of Khwarizm). Moscow, 1948

Wersin-Müller-Grah: *Das elementare Ornament und seine Gesetzlichkeit*. Ravensburg, 1940

V. N. Zasypkin: *Arkhitektura Srednei Azii* (The Architecture of Central Asia). Moscow, 1948

Enzyklopädie des Islam. Leipzig 1913, *Encyclopédie de l'Islam*, Nouvelle édition Paris, 1957

Zodchestvo Uzbekistana (The Architecture of Uzbekistan), ed. by the Academy of Sciences of Uzbekistan, Tashkent, 1959

2

3

5

6

7

8

9

12

13

14

15

16

19

20

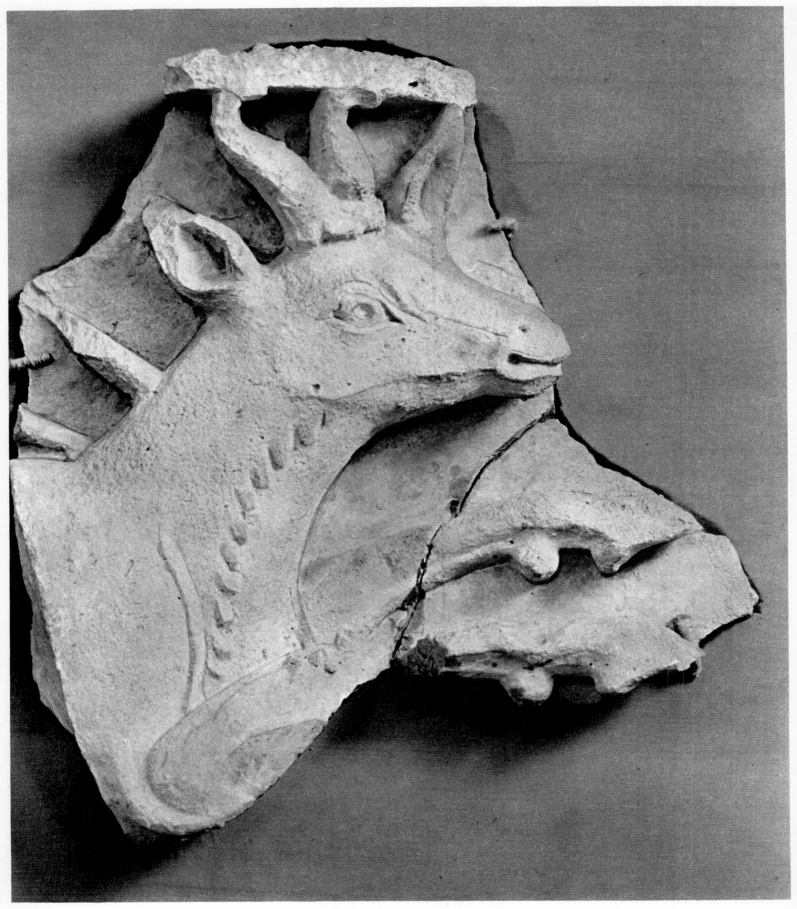

24

26

32

34

37

38

41

45

47

49

54

61

65

71

73

77

79

با امرا و نزدیکان خود گفت می کو یه مسئد میان ما و ثمالش شیه در میان است رای بابران کرد

و گفت از به دیبر خیل یزا رود در یا غوس شید کی دریا بی آتش که لشگر من پست بیگر فیلی بی آب به کسی گر

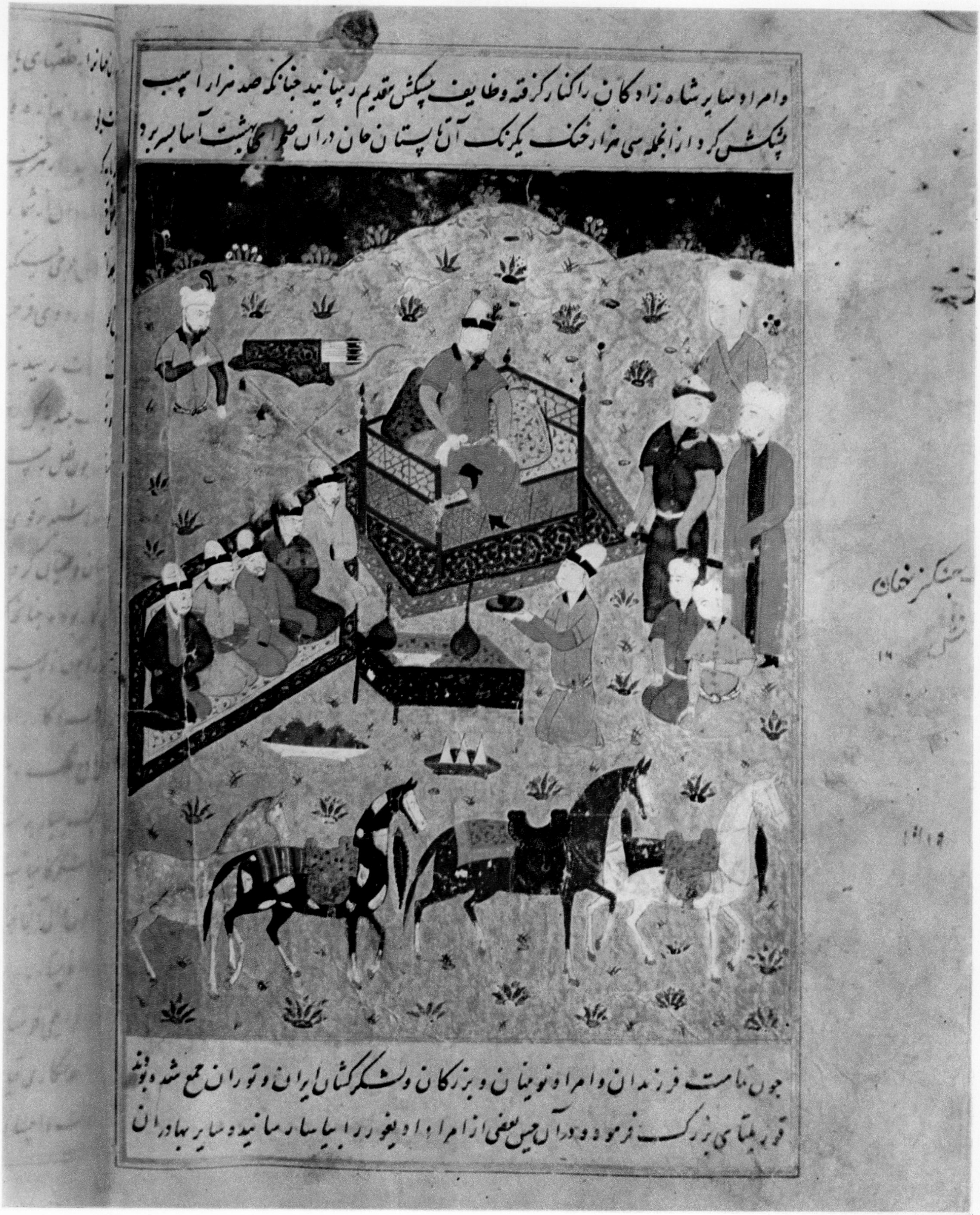

فرستاد وكفت اگرین پهلوان بدست نوكشته شود من يعف ملكت خود را ابوخواهم دادچون
ان كافريزه يك سلطان رسيد سلطان ... وزكار فذ كى كرس كرده پيكاي ... آب ... نهاده بروجار يز غفان
جوآورد دست پيلى رابكوش ... برآمد زشاخ كوزمان خروخوشى ... قضاكفت كيروقد زكفته ده
فلك آفرين كرد وكفت وزد ... جوبكدشت پيكان برانگشت او ... كذ كرد ازمهره پشت او
بهان يك ضرب تيراى كل فرمكود ... ازاسب اند زآمك نجاك سپيا د ... زخون ىل شده روى آورد كا ة
ان كافورا سرسه بسرو دبكين بهرايك يك درآمك نذ وبرد دست سلطان نگشته شد نذ ىمجنين ... تانه
پهلوان از كافوان كرجستان درميدان بغيا ذ مهابت سلطان در دل كافوان اثركرد سلطان نرب

كبرواضه واشارت بجانب لشكر ظفر پيكر كرد نام لشكر جلا ... وبزر خودرا به سلطان رسانيد ند دركاه

92

94

108

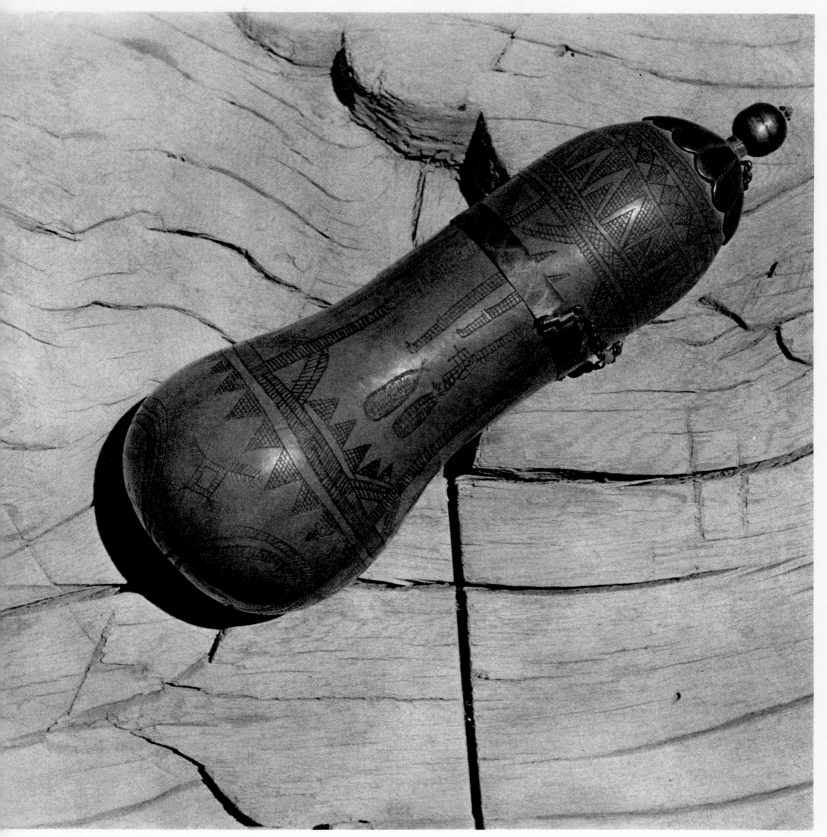

122

131